CORAL REEFS

BY

GAIL GIBBONS

SCHOLASTIC INC.
New York Toronto London Auckland Sydney
Mexico City New Delhi Hong Kong Buenos Aires

To Mary Cash

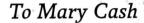

Special thanks to Dr. Kim Ritchie, marine biologist, and Nadine Slimak, public relations manager, at the Mote Marine Laboratory, Sarasota, Florida

The samples of sea life shown in this book are from coral reefs around the world. These plants and animals do not necessarily share the same habitat simultaneously as illustrated here. All the sea life shown in the Great Barrier Reef (pages 26–27) actually live there.

ISBN-13: 978-0-545-11018-1
ISBN-10: 0-545-11018-1

Copyright © 2007 by Gail Gibbons.
All rights reserved. Published by Scholastic Inc.,
557 Broadway, New York, NY 10012, by arrangement
with Holiday House, Inc. SCHOLASTIC and associated
logos are trademarks and/or registered trademarks
of Scholastic Inc.

12 11 10 9 8 7 6 5 4   10 11 12 13/0

Printed in the U.S.A.   08

First Scholastic printing, September 2008

Sunlight shines through seawater into a coral reef. The reef is an underwater world of brilliant colors and strange shapes.

3

Where Coral Reefs Are Found

MARINE BIOLOGISTS study the oceans and what lives in them.

Marine biologists believe coral reefs existed about 400 million years ago, when dinosaurs lived. At the same time that dinosaurs became extinct, coral reefs died out. About 50 million years ago coral reefs began to return, and they continue to survive.

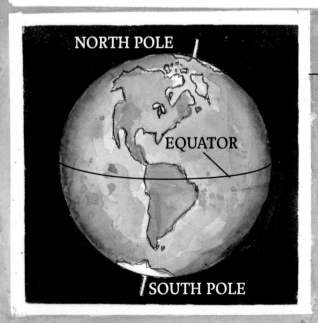

NORTH POLE

EQUATOR

SOUTH POLE

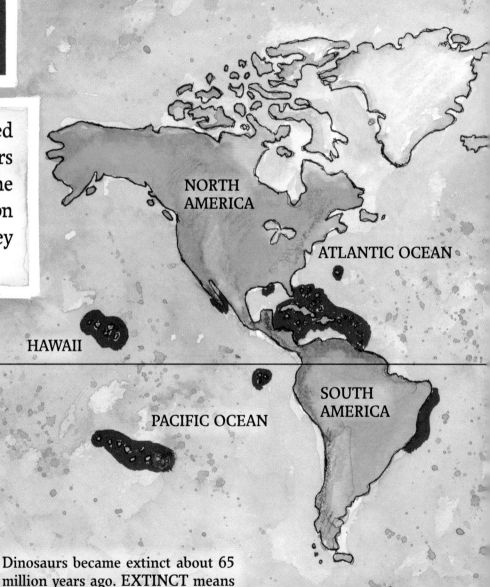

NORTH AMERICA

ATLANTIC OCEAN

HAWAII

SOUTH AMERICA

PACIFIC OCEAN

Dinosaurs became extinct about 65 million years ago. EXTINCT means to no longer exist.

An ECOSYSTEM is a community in nature, including all living and nonliving parts.

Coral reefs are found in shallow, unpolluted tropical waters near the equator. They are fragile and need a special ecosystem to survive. The water temperature usually is between 64° Fahrenheit (17.8° Celsius) and 88° Fahrenheit (31.1° Celsius).

EUROPE

PACIFIC OCEAN

ASIA

The EQUATOR is an imaginary line around the middle of Earth, equally distant from the North Pole and the South Pole.

AFRICA

INDIAN OCEAN

AUSTRALIA

ANTARCTICA

5

Marine biologists tell us that coral reefs were built over long periods of time with the tiny skeletons of animals called hard coral polyps.

DIADEM DOTTYBACKS

LEAFY CORAL

ANGLERFISH

ELKHORN CORAL

LONGSNOUT SEA HORSE

FINGER CORAL

Hard Coral Polyp Skeleton

When the hard coral polyp dies, the skeleton of the hard base remains. This becomes limestone.

CUP CORAL

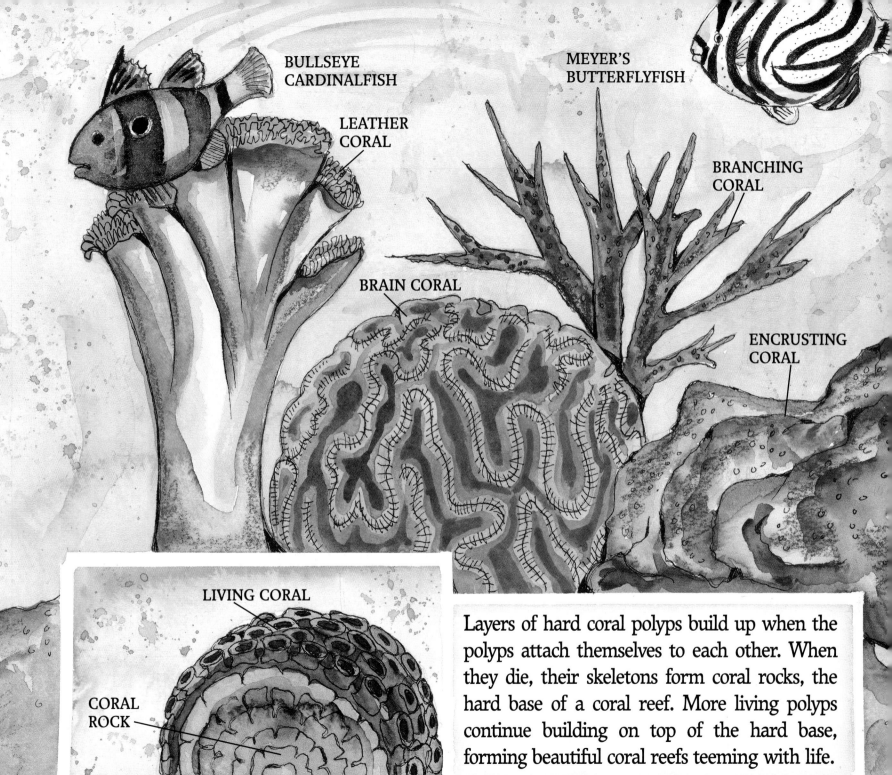

BULLSEYE
CARDINALFISH

LEATHER
CORAL

MEYER'S
BUTTERFLYFISH

BRANCHING
CORAL

ENCRUSTING
CORAL

BRAIN CORAL

LIVING CORAL

CORAL
ROCK

Layers of hard coral polyps build up when the polyps attach themselves to each other. When they die, their skeletons form coral rocks, the hard base of a coral reef. More living polyps continue building on top of the hard base, forming beautiful coral reefs teeming with life.

Three Kinds of Coral Reefs

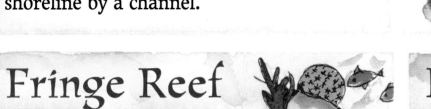

BLUE
DEVILFISH

A fringe reef grows close to the shoreline. A barrier reef grows farther away from the shoreline. It is separated from the shoreline by a channel.

Fringe Reef

Barrier Reef

SHORELINE

Fringe Reef

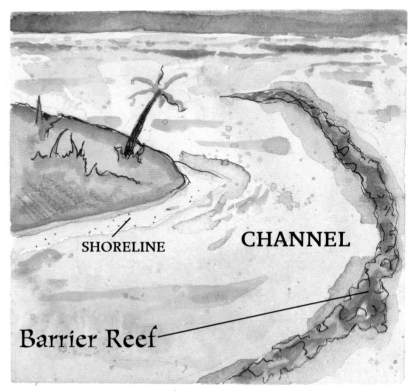

SHORELINE

CHANNEL

Barrier Reef

Atoll

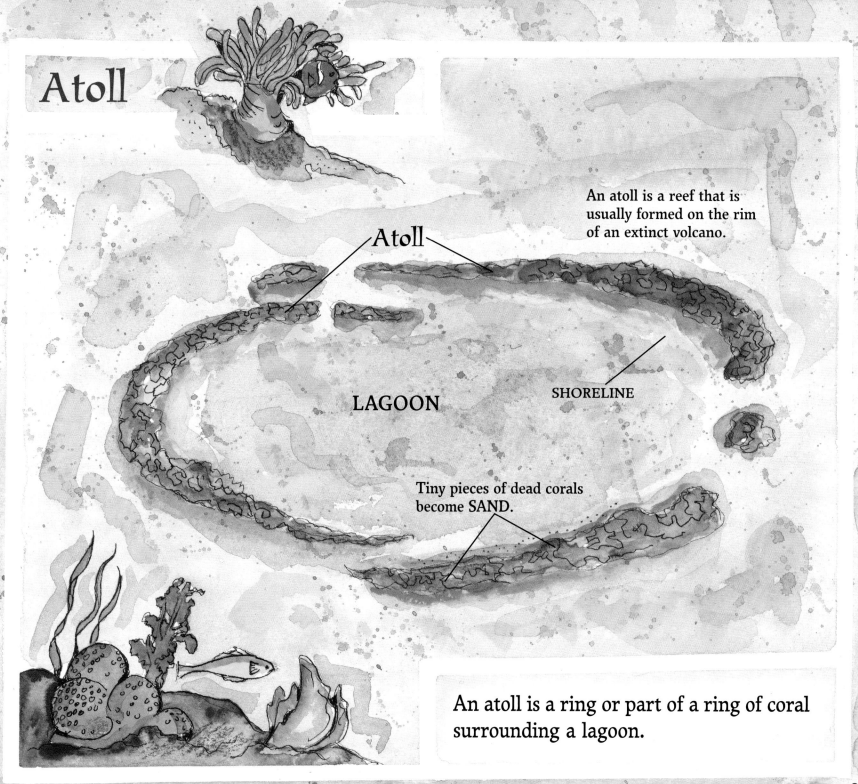

Atoll

An atoll is a reef that is usually formed on the rim of an extinct volcano.

SHORELINE

LAGOON

Tiny pieces of dead corals become SAND.

An atoll is a ring or part of a ring of coral surrounding a lagoon.

Coral Reef Zones

Different kinds of corals and sea life thrive in their own special places in a coral reef, called zones. Every reef can be divided into three zones.

Shore Zone

It is close to the shoreline, where the water is shallow.

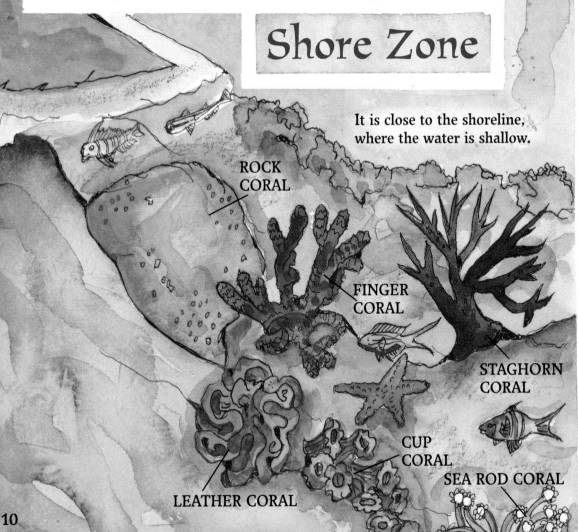

ROCK CORAL

FINGER CORAL

STAGHORN CORAL

CUP CORAL

SEA ROD CORAL

LEATHER CORAL

Crest Reef Zone

ELKHORN CORAL

BRAIN CORAL

STAR CORAL

The amount of sunlight and the motion of the sea vary in the three different zones of a coral reef. Sea life is most abundant at a depth of about 30 feet (9.1 meters) of water.

It is farther off the shoreline, where the water is the most shallow.

STAGHORN CORAL

Fore Reef Zone

It is farthest away from the shoreline, where the water is deeper than in the other zones.

BOULDER CORAL

SAWTOOTH BARRACUDA

FIRE CORAL

LETTUCE CORAL

PLATE CORAL

DROP-OFF SLOPE

LEAFY CORAL

COLUMN CORAL

CACTUS CORAL

SEA FAN CORAL

How Coral Reefs Grow

At certain times of the year, after a full moon, many corals in a reef release eggs into the seawater. The eggs soon become floating baby corals, called planulae (PLAN·yuh·lie). When a planula (PLAN·yuh·luh) attaches itself to a reef or a hard surface, it forms into a coral polyp.

A tiny oval larva of a coral polyp is called a PLANULA.

It uses its HAIRS to swim.

TOMATO ANEMONEFISH

CORAL EGG

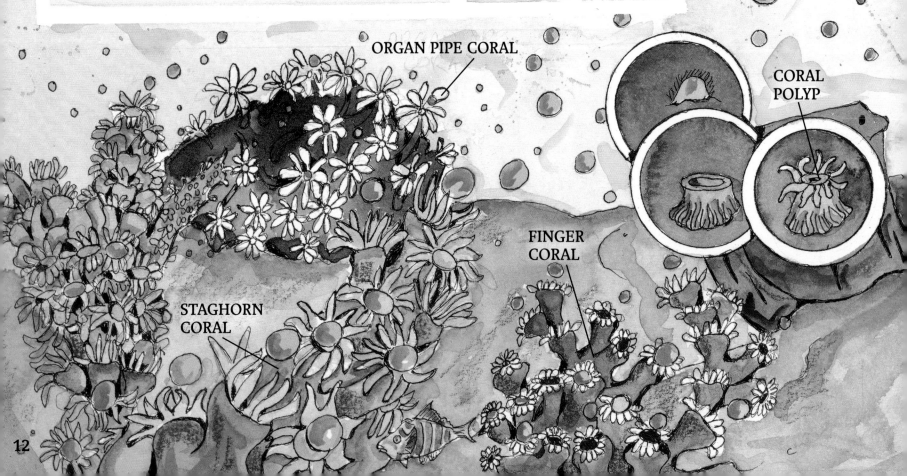

ORGAN PIPE CORAL

CORAL POLYP

FINGER CORAL

STAGHORN CORAL

SEA SLUG

BROAD-BANDED CARDINALFISH

CHOCOLATE SURGEONFISH

SEA ROD CORAL

Over time each coral polyp reproduces another polyp connected to it. Every new polyp does the same thing. Gradually the coral structure becomes larger and larger.

LONG-SPINED SEA URCHIN

ENCRUSTING CORAL

TUBE SPONGE

NEW CORAL POLYP

Hard and Soft Coral Polyps

A Hard Coral Polyp

A hard coral polyp is held in place by its hard cup base. Above the base its body is soft with stinging tentacles surrounding its edge. To protect itself it will pull its soft body and tentacles inside its hard cup base. There are about 650 known kinds of hard coral polyps.

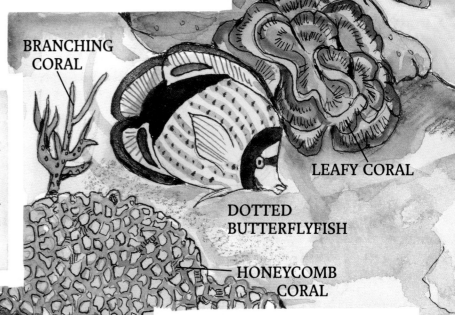

BANDED SEA SNAKE

BRANCHING CORAL

LEAFY CORAL

DOTTED BUTTERFLYFISH

HONEYCOMB CORAL

MUSHROOM CORAL

STAR CORAL

RUBY BRITTLE STAR

Hard Coral Polyp

TENTACLES are used for protection and to catch prey.

MOUTH

SOFT BODY

HARD CUP BASE

14

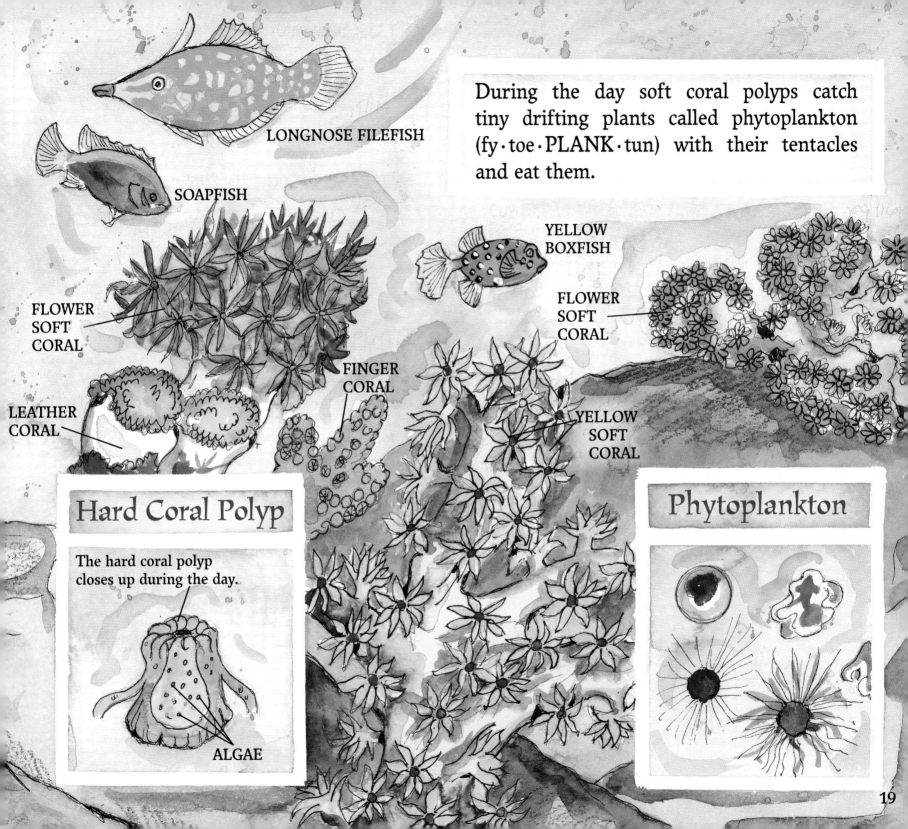

LONGNOSE FILEFISH

SOAPFISH

During the day soft coral polyps catch tiny drifting plants called phytoplankton (fy·toe·PLANK·tun) with their tentacles and eat them.

YELLOW BOXFISH

FLOWER SOFT CORAL

FLOWER SOFT CORAL

FINGER CORAL

YELLOW SOFT CORAL

LEATHER CORAL

Hard Coral Polyp

The hard coral polyp closes up during the day.

ALGAE

Phytoplankton

Nighttime on a Coral Reef

Most hard coral polyps eat only during the night. They catch extremely small animals called zooplankton (zoe·uh·PLANK·tun) with their tentacles and eat them. The soft coral polyps continue to eat during the night.

BLUE-RINGED OCTOPUS

YELLOW SEA WHIP CORAL

ORANGE SOFT CORAL

ENCRUSTING CORAL

FINGER CORAL

Zooplankton

REEF WHITETIP SHARK

CUP CORAL

MASSIVE CORAL

Phytoplankton and zooplankton cannot be seen without a microscope.

CUTTLEFISH

MANTA RAY

FEATHER STAR CORAL

BARRED MORAY EEL

LEATHER CORAL

PINK TREE CORAL

COLUMN CORAL

BUBBLE CORAL

CORAL CRAB

TABLE CORAL

CHRISTMAS TREE WORM

RED CAVE CORAL

Hard Coral Polyp

STAGHORN CORAL

The reef is colorful during the day, but it is at its most colorful at nighttime, when both the hard and soft coral polyps are open.

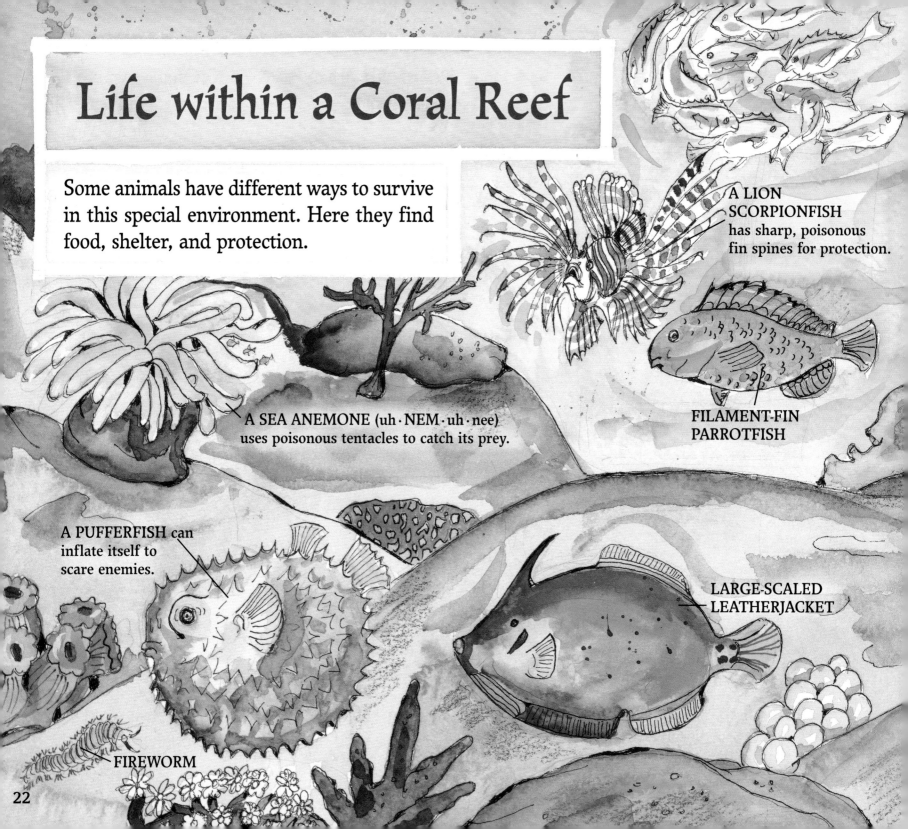

Life within a Coral Reef

Some animals have different ways to survive in this special environment. Here they find food, shelter, and protection.

A LION SCORPIONFISH has sharp, poisonous fin spines for protection.

A SEA ANEMONE (uh·NEM·uh·nee) uses poisonous tentacles to catch its prey.

FILAMENT-FIN PARROTFISH

A PUFFERFISH can inflate itself to scare enemies.

LARGE-SCALED LEATHERJACKET

FIREWORM

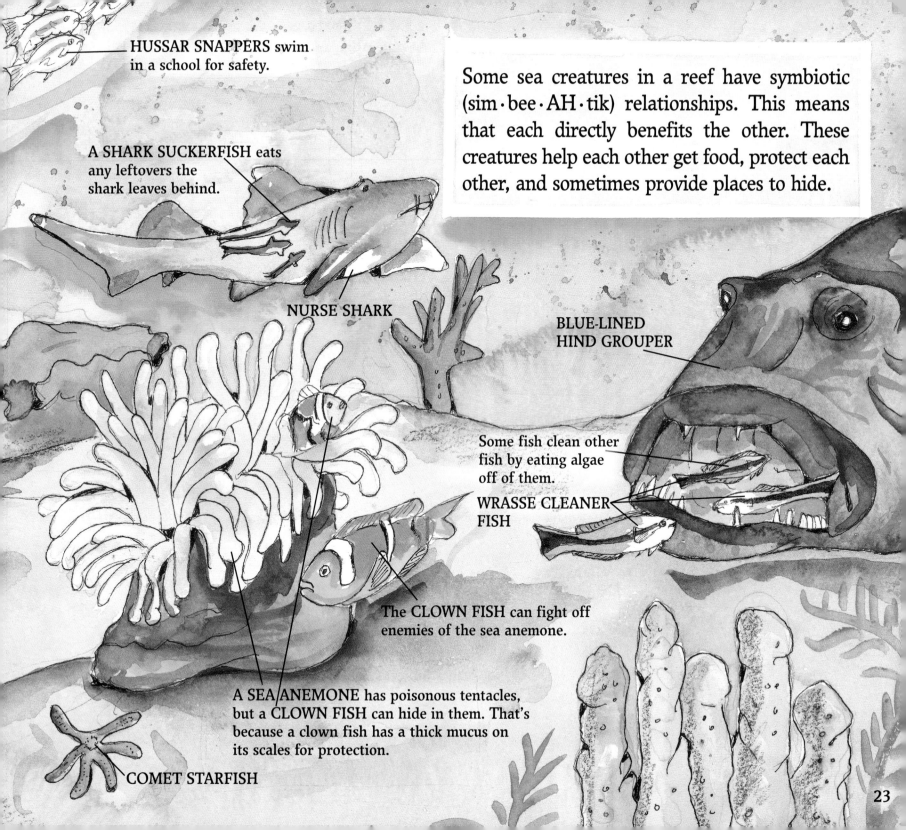

HUSSAR SNAPPERS swim in a school for safety.

A SHARK SUCKERFISH eats any leftovers the shark leaves behind.

NURSE SHARK

Some sea creatures in a reef have symbiotic (sim·bee·AH·tik) relationships. This means that each directly benefits the other. These creatures help each other get food, protect each other, and sometimes provide places to hide.

BLUE-LINED HIND GROUPER

Some fish clean other fish by eating algae off of them.

WRASSE CLEANER FISH

The CLOWN FISH can fight off enemies of the sea anemone.

A SEA ANEMONE has poisonous tentacles, but a CLOWN FISH can hide in them. That's because a clown fish has a thick mucus on its scales for protection.

COMET STARFISH

23

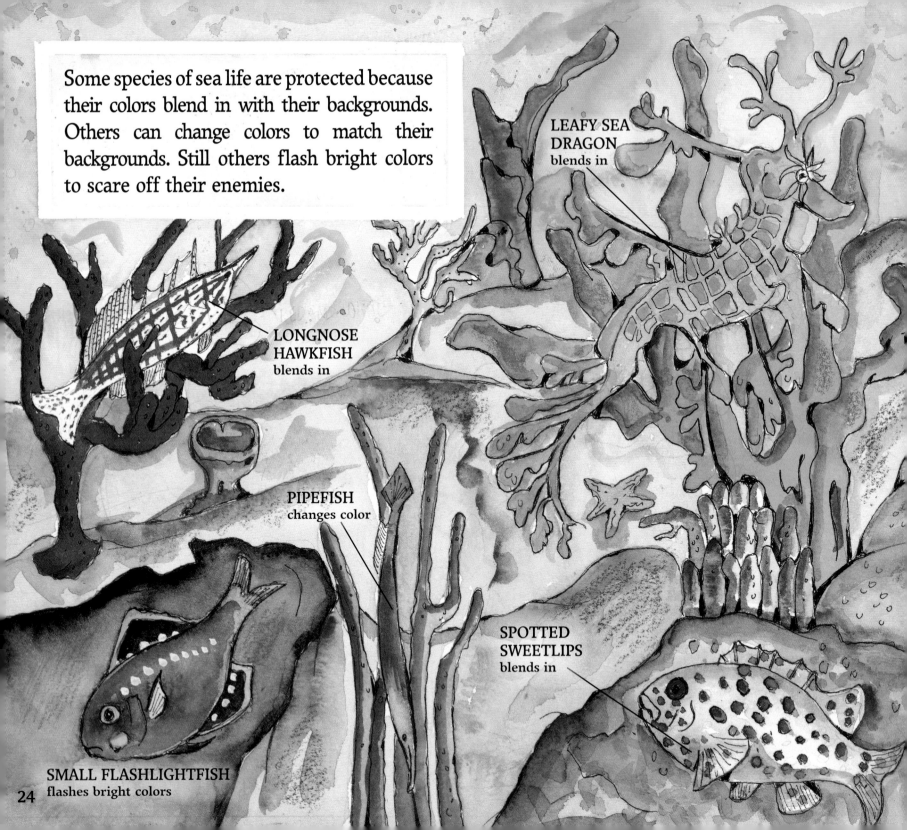

Some species of sea life are protected because their colors blend in with their backgrounds. Others can change colors to match their backgrounds. Still others flash bright colors to scare off their enemies.

LEAFY SEA DRAGON
blends in

LONGNOSE HAWKFISH
blends in

PIPEFISH
changes color

SPOTTED SWEETLIPS
blends in

SMALL FLASHLIGHTFISH
flashes bright colors

24

Daytime

BLUE DEVILFISH

YELLOW-SADDLE GOATFISH

REGAL ANGELFISH

TOMATO ANEMONEFISH

BLACK TRIGGERFISH

GREEN PARROTFISH

CUSHION SEA STAR

BROWN-BARRED GOBY

Nighttime

GREEN SEA TURTLE

SANDBAR SHARK

MANTA RAY

GIANT BARRACUDA

BARRED MORAY EEL

A coral reef is a very busy place during the day. About two-thirds of all the reef creatures are active at this time. Others hide during the day and feed at night.

The Great Barrier Reef

The largest coral reef in the world lies off the east coast of Australia. The reef is about 1,430 miles (2,301 kilometers) long. The Great Barrier Reef is so large that astronauts can see it from outer space.

BENGAL SERGEANT DAMSELFISH

SEA SLUG

SPINY ROW CORAL

RACCOON BUTTERFLYFISH

MASSIVE CORAL

TUBE SPONGE

GIANT CLAM

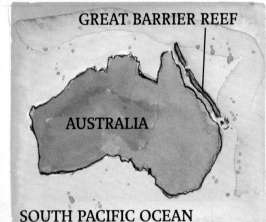

GREAT BARRIER REEF

AUSTRALIA

SOUTH PACIFIC OCEAN

CONE SNAIL

STAR CORAL

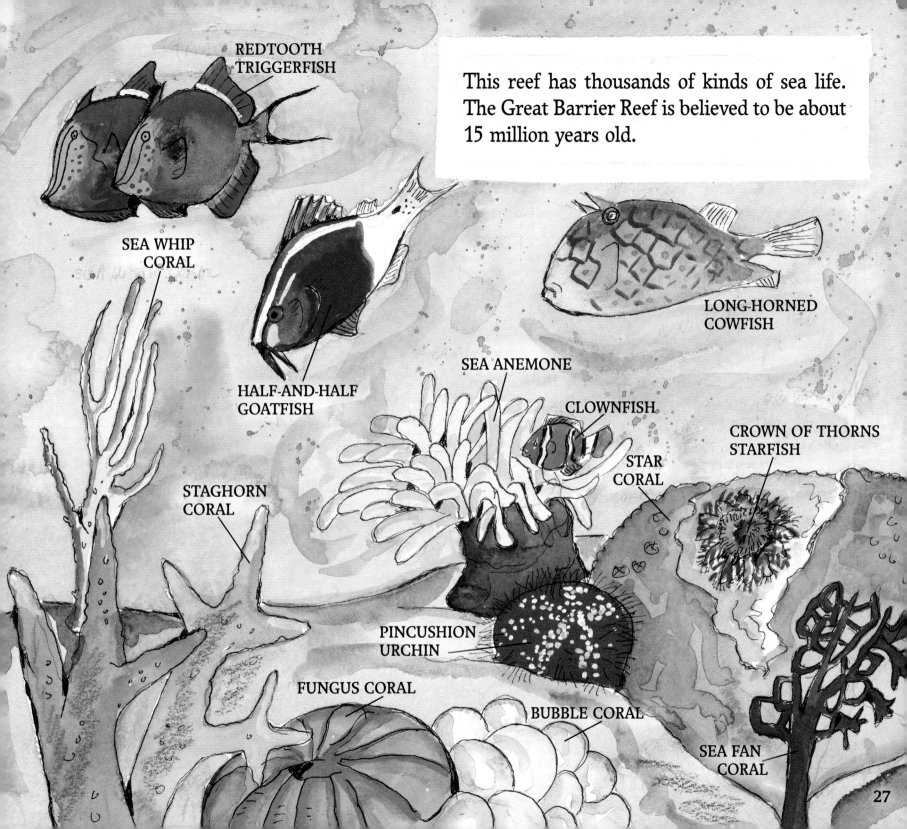

REDTOOTH TRIGGERFISH

This reef has thousands of kinds of sea life. The Great Barrier Reef is believed to be about 15 million years old.

SEA WHIP CORAL

LONG-HORNED COWFISH

HALF-AND-HALF GOATFISH

SEA ANEMONE

CLOWNFISH

STAR CORAL

CROWN OF THORNS STARFISH

STAGHORN CORAL

PINCUSHION URCHIN

FUNGUS CORAL

BUBBLE CORAL

SEA FAN CORAL

27

Look . . . but Don't Disturb!

Marine parks have been created to protect coral reefs. Some people use snorkels and others use scuba-diving equipment to explore the reefs.

SNORKEL

MASK

FLIPPERS

DO NOT TOUCH OR TAKE ANYTHING FROM THE REEF!

28

Coral reefs need to be protected. They actually help reduce global warming by taking carbon dioxide from the air and creating oxygen for all to breathe. Coral reefs everywhere are fragile and should not be disturbed.

GLOBAL WARMING is the rise in the world's temperature.

CARBON DIOXIDE is a gas that in large quantities pollutes the air.

Warmer seawater temperatures cause corals to die.

SCUBA TANK

MASK

WET SUIT

FLIPPERS

Many people like to visit sea aquariums to see coral reef exhibits.

EXHIBITS →

STING RAYS

Coral reefs are among the most beautiful and unusual places in the natural world. It is both fun and important to learn about them.

Coral Reefs

More sea creatures live in and around coral reefs than anywhere in the world's oceans.

Coral reefs are hard. Throughout history many ships sank when they ran into coral reefs.

About 200,000 kinds of plants and animal life that live within coral reefs have been discovered and named.

The United States has only one percent of all known coral reefs.

Marine biologists believe there could be as many as 2,000,000 types of sea life inhabiting the world's coral reefs.

Australia, the Philippines, and Indonesia have about half of all known coral reefs.

Papahānaumokuākea Marine National Monument

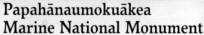

A giant clam can grow to be more than 4 feet (1.2 meters) wide and can weigh more than 500 pounds (226.8 kilograms).

In 2006 the United States designated the area around the Northwestern Hawaiian Islands a marine national monument. In 2007 it was renamed the Papahānaumokuākea (PAH-pah-HA-naoo-MOW-koo-a-KAY-uh) Marine National Monument. This monument includes 140,000 square miles (about 363,000 square kilometers) of ocean, islands, and reefs, an area larger than all U.S. national parks combined.

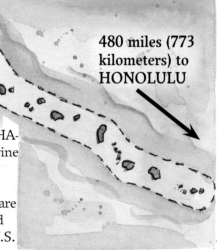

480 miles (773 kilometers) to HONOLULU

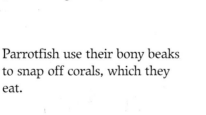

Parrotfish use their bony beaks to snap off corals, which they eat.